SPONTANEOUS COMBUSTION

A WRITER'S PRIMER FOR CREATIVE REVIVAL

NANCY BUTTS

ISBN: 1484032861
ISBN-13: 978-1484032862

In memory of my dad

But since it falls unto my lot
That I should rise and you should not
I'll gently rise and I'll softly call
Good night and joy be with you all

[Lyrics from "The Parting Glass"]

CONTENTS

Though the advice in this book may be couched in language that seems more slanted towards writers of fiction, everything it says can be applied to writers of non-fiction as well. So no matter what you write, read on.

1
WRITING REVIVAL

Why bother to read yet another book on writing?

Magnified by loudspeakers, the voice reverberated through a summer evening so hot that even the fireflies had given up on their usual twilight dance. Though I was half a mile away in my back yard, I could still hear every word the tent revival preacher said as he exhorted backsliders to "come afire again" with the love of the Lord.

Revivals such as this are a fixture of the small-town South where I've lived and worked as a writer since I graduated from college. But what does a tent revival have to do with a book on writing?

For that matter, why even bother to read yet another book on writing? What could I possibly have to say that would add anything to the wisdom already offered by writers the caliber of Stephen King, John Gardner, Dorothea Brande, Brenda Ueland, Natalie Goldberg, Anne Lamott, Les Edgerton, and so many more?

> **spontaneous combustion**
> |spɑnˈteɪniəs kəmˈbəstʃən|
> *noun*
> the ignition of organic matter without apparent cause, typically through heat generated internally by rapid oxidation.

The answer, I hope, lies in the phrase above: a special kind of internal ignition. That's what this book is about—how writers can spontaneously combust; how they, like the backsliders in the revival tent, can come afire again—not with the love of the Lord, but with the love of writing. What I hope to do in these pages is help you find the resolve to keep writing in the face of what often seems like nonstop resistance from life, the universe, and everything.

I've had some extremely modest success as a newspaper reporter, freelance writer, children's author, book editor, speaker, writing teacher, and manuscript consultant. But what does that experience give me to share that you couldn't find elsewhere?

Absolutely nothing.

I'm not sure there is anything new under the sun. I think many of the books on the craft of writing are repackaging the same ideas. And there is nothing wrong with that. Just as there are a limited number of plots in the world of fiction, so too are there a limited number of things anyone can tell you about the mechanics of creating fiction: whether that be building a plot, creating characters, developing conflict, or anything else. Likewise, there are a limited number of things anyone can tell you about the mechanics of researching and writing compelling non-fiction.

The difference between one book about writing and the next isn't the content itself then, it's the way that content is expressed. That's great for writers, because not all of us learn the same way.

It's like religion. Some people connect with the divine better when they hear it in Latin or Greek or Old Church Slavonic. Others can only hear the divine in the voice of a charismatic speaking in tongues, a mother blessing Sabbath candles—or a revival preacher booming through the sullen air of a summer evening.

It's the same with writers. Some, for example, get the most out of an academic treatise analyzing the three-act structure of novels. Others prefer to read about a specific system for plotting, whether that's based on mythic journeys, saving a cat, colored index cards, or snowflakes.

But some people find all of this too stifling, even constipating creatively. What they seek is inspiration.

And whether they taste success or not—whether they get a crumb at that table or an entire banquet— eventually all writers need to replenish their depleted stores of wisdom and inspiration and energy.

That's why we can always squeeze another book on writing onto our already-overcrowded shelves. Because writers need revivals, too. Revivals speak to an eternal human need; we all need replenishment, we all need filling up.

Let me tell you a story. In my years of teaching, I've had the privilege of working with thousands of students, helping them fulfill their writing dreams. But one particular student stands out in my memory.

In his first letter to me, he introduced himself as a husband, stay-at-home father—and a failed screenwriter. Those are the exact words he used.

Failed. Writer.

I'm not sure if this was a judgment that was levied by someone else—some college professor or self-anointed expert in the film industry—or a label he had applied to himself. But those words haunted me. With a poison like that circulating through his mind, how could he ever hope to write?

It was with a sense of dread that I read his first story. What if it was as bad as he said? How could I be the one to add another voice to the damning, accusatory chorus in his head?

I almost cried with relief when I read his first assignment. His story was luminous: a moving vignette about a young girl on a school bus. It showed a warm, gentle insight into the heart of this child, and in gem-like prose that proved—to me, at least—that he was a true artist with language. He was the furthest thing from a failure.

I spent the next few years trying to convince him of that, to get him to see in himself what I saw. In dozens of letters and manuscript edits and emails I used every word I could find to encourage him and buoy him up as a writer.

But sadly, I couldn't. I was never able to shout down whatever voice it was he carried around in his head that was always taunting…

Failed. Writer.

He is why I am writing this book. Because in my years of teaching and editing, I have encountered legions of people like him—writers at every stage of their careers, from novice to published pro—who need revival. They…you…we need to remember who we are, and what our purpose is in chasing our writing dreams.

We need to hold our own tent revival. Though the scripture may never change, we still need to hear the same truths repeated, over and over, about why we write. Each of us keeps searching, keeps circling back, to soak up another verse of literary wisdom. Each time we hear something different, as if it were new.

May you hear a voice in this book that gives you what you need to ignite your own writer's revival.

2
CLOTHES ARE ENTIRELY OPTIONAL

Writing isn't an indulgence

"Take your writing seriously,
because nobody else will."

This advice from my editor Stephen Roxburgh is the mantra, the litany, that informs this chapter and indeed, this entire book. I believe that our failure to do this—to take our writing seriously, to consider it as valuable and meaningful as all the other activities in our lives—is the key to why we don't write. Changing that is the goal of this book.

• This isn't a book about craft.

• This isn't a book about publishing or marketing. [Though there is a definite need for such books, especially now that electronic publishing offers whole new possibilities and perils for writers and their work.]

• This isn't a book about how to manage the business of being a writer.

This book is about none of those things. Rather, it is about how to live as a writer: how to *be* a writer on a daily basis.

This is harder than it sounds. Being a writer every day requires more than just deciding to get up and write. How many New Year's resolutions have you made that this is the year you'll finally start that novel? Is it finished yet? If you're reading this book, I'd wager it isn't.

How many times have you told yourself that once you've finished

[fill in the blank _____]

painting the bedroom
cleaning the basement
doing your taxes
clearing away that big project at work
visiting your in-laws
taking a vacation to recover after visiting your in-laws

....you'll finally have time to work on your book?

8

But somehow you never find your way to your desk, and nothing—or very little—ever gets written.

Look, I've been there—in fact, I am there now. I am always there. I have this endless list in my head of things that I'm convinced I have to accomplish every morning when I get out of bed before I can even think about writing. You probably have a similar list: get up, take a shower, get dressed, make the bed, feed the dog, take him out, make breakfast, wash the dishes, start a load of laundry, run to the grocery, post office, library, bank, gas station…and on and on and on.

The question you need to ask yourself is this: why are those things more important to you than writing? Because if you're doing them first, they're more important. OK, feed the dog so he doesn't eat you, but everything else is optional—even clothes. The French writer Colette wrote naked.

[Though the reason why she wrote naked might make you feel better about your writerly procrastination. Colette apparently had such a dread of facing the blank page that her husband took away her clothes and locked her in her office for three hours every morning, to force her to write. We'll talk about that dread later, in chapter 6, because it is one of the major reasons that writers avoid writing.]

But don't try to wriggle away from the uncomfortable question I asked earlier: why do you let everything else in your life overshadow your writing? If you want to write as much as you believe, then why do you so rarely sit down and actually do it?

I don't think it's just an issue of time management. Yes, we are all busy, often insanely so. We all have places we are expected to be, things we are expected to do—like earn a living!—and people we are expected to take care of.

And these aren't always burdens imposed on us from others either; frequently we are the ones putting the most pressure on ourselves to meet a laundry list of obligations, commitments, and responsibilities. We may even love doing these things, and derive an intense sense of meaning and joy from doing them.

I certainly cannot sit here and tell you to drop all that as if it were a vial of Ebola virus. But I do have to deliver some unwelcome news. If you really want to write, something is going to have to go. You cannot have it all; no one can. We all have to steal time from other essential, productive, and pleasurable activities in order to write. [Sleep is often the first thing you have to kiss good-bye.]

And though it may make you grind your teeth in a kind of furious, resentful envy, there are people out there who do manage to write, and write prolifically, with all the same obligations that you have. *Grr*!

If they can do it, why aren't you?

Once again, why is everything else in your life more important to you than writing? Because if you find that you aren't writing even when you think you want to, then the logical conclusion is that writing isn't actually as important to you as you believe.

Or is it?

Perhaps the reason you aren't writing is not that *you* consider it unimportant, but that you believe other people think it's unimportant. There is a subtle but essential difference between the two, one that I think is at the heart of why writers don't write—why we can't seem to spontaneously combust.

To me, being a writer starts with valuing yourself not just as a person, but specifically as a writer. Before you can write a single word, you have to believe deep down in the mitochondria of your cells that writing is a valid use of your time.

Writing isn't selfish, it isn't lazy, it isn't indulgent, and it isn't a waste of time or energy.

Repeat that to yourself a couple of hundred times. And then say it once more for good measure.

But your perfervid writer's imagination is in overdrive. In your mind you are writing dialogue for everyone in your life, from your mother-in-law to your co-workers to strangers on the street. And what you hear them saying is this, "You're not curing cancer. You're not getting a paycheck. And after three hours slaving away over a hot computer, you don't even have a casserole to show for it. What a colossal waste of time."

This soundtrack of disapproving, disappointed voices in your head convinces you that you were wrong to ever believe that your writing could be significant or meaningful. Your writing can't be important because no one else thinks it is.

And let's not forget the kids who keep needing to be fed three times a day, even though you just fed them the day before. They need feeding and holding and loving and comforting and guiding and tending, and that's a pure and perfect and noble purpose, and of course you should do it, and of course you want to do it....

But if you don't believe that writing is also a legitimate, noble, meaningful thing to do as well, you'll feel as guilty about your writing time as you do scarfing down an entire pint of Ben & Jerry's ice cream—and ultimately, you'll stop writing entirely.

So I'll say it again. In order to write, you have to stop echoing other people's judgments. You have to stop basing your evaluation of the importance of your writing on whether anybody else thinks it is. You have to convince yourself of the value and meaning of what you are doing as a writer.

Because when you are convinced that your writing is important, you will make time for it, no matter what.

Because I'm a woman, and a mother, it might seem like many of the specific examples in this book are aimed primarily at other women and moms. And it may be that women have a harder time honoring and respecting their own creative drives. Virginia Woolf certainly thought so, as she wrote in her classic book *A Room of One's Own*.

A writer and poet named Tillie Olsen whom you've probably never heard of thought so, too. At the tender age of 19, Olsen received a publishing contract from Random House for a novel based on a single chapter that she'd written.

On the day she died at the age of 94, Olsen still hadn't finished that novel. It was crowded out of her life by the responsibilities of holding down a job, raising her children, and keeping a home. Decades later, she did publish four short stories, one of which, "Tell Me a Riddle," won the O. Henry Prize. She taught at several colleges and won a Guggenheim Fellowship, so it's not as if her life was a waste.

But she never finished that novel. And the success she ultimately had came only after decades of silence. In fact, one of her most famous books, *Silences*, is about this very thing.

As Olsen and so many other writers—both men and women—have discovered, the reality is that writing time has to compete with family time, and relationship time, and job time. And time—along with energy, both physical and creative—is a finite resource. In choosing to write, you will have to sacrifice in some other arena of your life.

I know how incredibly difficult that is to do, and at many points in my own life, I chose not to do it. I chose to put someone or something else in my life above writing. Whether I was right or wrong to make that choice, the fact remains that at those moments, I was tacitly proclaiming that I didn't believe in the value of my writing, not enough to make it a priority.

After I had published my first novel, *Cheshire Moon*, I asked my editor if he thought it was a good investment in my career to spend what seemed to me to be a lot of money to attend my first national conference as a published children's author out in Los Angeles.

Stephen's answer was an unequivocal yes. I've forgotten the exact words he used, so I'm paraphrasing here, but he said the words that began this chapter. "You have to take your writing seriously, because no one else will."

Look carefully at what he said. He did not say take *yourself* seriously; therein likes the road to alienating everyone around you with your pompous self-regard. What he said is that you should take what you *do* seriously: that is, write.

In the years since then, I've learned the hard way that my editor was right: all too often, nobody else does take my writing seriously.

Once when I was on a plane, flying to Connecticut to teach a course for other writers, the man in the seat next to me wanted to trade business cards. Fortunately I had some, dashed off on my printer just the night before. "Nancy Butts, Author," they read, with the titles of my two YA novels beneath.

He glanced at the card for a second, then frowned as if he didn't get the punch line to a joke I'd just told. "No, really," he said. "What do you do?"

And just try filling out a loan application; see what looks you get from the loan officer when you fill in your occupation as "self-employed writer."

Moments like these certainly don't make it easy to take your writing seriously. If you're not earning at least a five-figure income from it, if agents and editors aren't burning up your cell phone minutes trying to sign you, if—like the Scarecrow in Oz—you don't have a "testimonial" like an award or a spot on somebody's best-seller list, then the world doesn't respect what you do. It doesn't consider the time you spend writing a worthwhile investment.

Ignore the world. Dig down and find the value of what you do within yourself.

The only way to do that is simply to keep writing.

Obviously, I'm preaching to myself more than just a little here, to remind myself that what I do has significance.

If writing is such a worthy purpose, then I need to get up every morning and make it my priority. And so do you. In chapters 4, 5, 7, and 8, I'm going to talk about some specific things you can do to help put your writing firmly at the center of your life.

And for the past few weeks, I've been doing just that. I go to bed at night auditioning sentences and ideas for this book, and the first thing I do when I get out of bed, even before I brush my teeth, is come to my computer and write those sentences down. I even forget to eat breakfast until I look up at the clock and see that it is nearly time for lunch.

Now you try. Postpone that bowl of cereal until you've written a paragraph that describes what your cat is doing on the fire escape. Take off your earphones, pull out a piece of paper, and jot down the conversation you can't help but overhear from the seat behind you in the bus. Dictate ideas for a scene into your smartphone while you're waiting in the car pool line at school.

Come afire again with love for writing; that's what I want for all of you who are reading this book.

The first step is convincing yourself that writing is a worthy pursuit. What makes it such a noble calling? Let's explore that in the next chapter.

3
WHY WRITE?

Only a story will mend it

I cried when I read the first review of my debut novel. Now that may have had something to do with the fact that I'd just had a terrifying glitch with the cruise control in my car. It refused to switch off as I was racing towards an intersection at 55 miles per hour. Obviously, I survived, or I wouldn't be here to write this book. But I was already a little shaky when I read the review.

Still, I think I would have been upset about it anyway. It wasn't the five-star glowing review I'd always fantasized about, and I was completely blinded to the good things it did say. All I saw, or remembered, were the things the reviewer didn't like.

It took me a while to get over that. And it took even longer for me to realize this: you can't rely on the world to validate your work, not even the literary world.

Especially not the literary world. Agents, editors, critics, reviewers, and readers aren't always going to understand what you are trying to say [once you've managed to finish writing it, that is], much less agree with it. So you have to cultivate the certainty within yourself that what you have written, and what you will write, has meaning regardless of what anyone else thinks about it.

What that meaning or purpose is will be different for every writer. The thing that drives you to write— the thing that ignites that wondrous process of spontaneous combustion—is something only you can know. But I think what gives writing significance to those of us who do it falls roughly into five categories.

❧ Expression: This is often denigrated as "writing as therapy," but to me, expression means far more than mere emotional venting. I think this is the fundamental reason anyone writes about anything, whether fiction or non-fiction. In every book, from novels to cookbooks, there is some underlying truth or value, some perception or judgment or attitude towards the world, that the writer is trying to express.

Why Write?

🌑 Entertainment: Sometimes a cigar is just a cigar. In other words, sometimes a writer creates a book primarily to give readers a laugh, or to make them cry along with a pair of star-crossed lovers, or to take them along on a fast-paced adventure. I still think self-expression creeps into these books as well, whether the writer intends it or not. Theme is sneaky that way.

🌑 Education: A lot of non-fiction books fall into this category [not all though; think of memoirs], but even fiction can teach something as well. I am most definitely *not* talking about novels or stories with a blatant "moral" or message; don't get me started on that rant. Think more of books like science fiction based on quantum physics, or thrillers based on medicine and the law.

🌑 Exhortation: A vegan doesn't just write that cookbook to share tasty recipes; whether she comes out and says it or not, she's also expressing her belief in the health or compassion of her dietary choices, and trying to convince you to follow suit. Many religious, inspirational, and self-help books fall into this category as well. They often combine exhortation with another E: encouragement.

🌑 Escape: It isn't just readers who yearn to escape the cares and burdens of their lives by immersing themselves in the world of a book. For writers, creating that story world can be the best escape hatch ever.

Remember, when I introduced these five categories I said they were rough ones. I'm sure there are other creative drives that I've overlooked; and in most books, some combination of these five motives is present. In fact, I think I am expressing, exhorting/encouraging, and educating all at once in this book. [And let's be honest: I'm escaping as well.]

And I'm sure many of you have caught the omission in this list. I intentionally left out "wanting to make money" as a category here, and not just because I couldn't fit it into my alliterative list of E's either. Of course you want to be able to make a living at what you love, but I don't consider that a creative drive; it's a financial one.

It is true that some of our most beloved and enduring works were the product of pressing financial need. Charles Dickens wrote many of his books—including *The Christmas Carol*—in a rush, on deadline, in order to make money to support his extensive family. That doesn't make his books any less creative or worthwhile or compelling.

But I would still caution you: if the *only* reason you take your writing seriously is because you see it as a way to make money, you are setting yourself up for disappointment. The brutal reality is that most writers have to work at something else in order to support their desire to write.

You can't rely on the world to assign meaning to your work as a writer; you have to forge your sense of writing purpose yourself.

It may help you to articulate your reasons for writing by hearing mine, so let me share the goal that drives me when I sit down to write.

It is summed up in two quotes that I keep prominently on my computer. Taken together, they express my belief—my faith—that Story, with a capital S, is one of the central ways that human beings are able to find meaning in the bewildering experiences of life.

"Only connect."
~EM Forster

"When the bond between heaven and earth is broken, even prayer is not enough; only a story can mend it."
~Ba'al Shem Tov

Forster was an English novelist famous for books such as *Howard's End*, *A Passage to India*, and *A Room with a View*. The Ba'al Shem Tov was an 18th-century Hasidic rabbi. Two very different men separated by time and culture, but I think they are both expressing the same truth. Writing gives you the opportunity to touch people whom you will never meet—and to do so in a way that can help them to make sense of their world, and to maintain their equilibrium as they attempt to navigate it.

I also believe that fiction can accomplish this far better than the more explicit, direct, in-your-face manner that you find in either sermons or self-help books.

"Storytelling reveals meaning without committing the error of defining it."
~Hannah Arendt, historian

"Our species thinks in metaphors and learns through stories."
~Mary Catherine Bateson, anthropologist

What these quotes affirm for me is that sometimes we have to write *around* the truth in order to best convey it. We have to embody truths about life in our characters and the things that happen to them. Their triumphs and tragedies, though fictional, take straighter aim into the hearts and minds of readers than any unvarnished fact could ever do.

In the 1990's television series *Northern Exposure* there is a recurring character named Leonard Quinhagak, a native American shaman, or healer, in the quirky Alaska town in which the series is set. The local doctor and main protagonist, Joel Fleischman, is a firm believer in the power of Western medicine, and bristles at first when his patients call on Leonard instead.

But Leonard doesn't see himself as being in competition with Joel. I vividly remember one bar scene where Leonard explained what he did. He said that in order to cure his patients of the ills they were experiencing, he first had to get to know them—so he could discover the true Story of their lives, and tell it to them. Once they heard their Story, and embraced it, they would be healed.

That is why I write: because I hope that in some small way I can be like Leonard, too. In connecting with my characters, uncovering their stories and sharing them in my books, perhaps readers I will never know can have an "aha!" moment and recognize their Story—and thus be healed.

This is why, with so many other things competing for my energy and attention, I believe that writing is a meaningful and worthwhile way to spend my time.

So why is your writing valuable to you? In years of working with other writers, I've heard many reasons. But to me, they all come down to one word: *share*. I believe most writers are driven to write by a burning need to share something with others that is deeply significant to them.

❦ To leave a legacy for children and grandchildren
❦ To permanently record oral history, often from a family member

23

❧ To interpret and explain the events of one's own life in the form of a memoir

❧ To teach others

❧ To help others in some way

❧ To spread the tenets of one's religion or belief system

❧ To remind the world of something you think it has forgotten, or needs to hear

❧ To convey some truth you've learned about life

Although in my list of the Five E's I talked about both entertainment and escape as reasons to write, it's rare that I've heard someone say that either one of these was their sole reason for writing. There is usually something else—something from the list above—that creeps into their books as well.

Note also that the list above applies equally well to both fiction and non-fiction. Most fiction is infused with themes that, to paraphrase Hannah Arendt, reveal meaning without making the error of defining it. This is another way of saying that you don't need to write about facts in order to convey deep layers of truth.

You might think first of heavyweight classics or prizewinners when I say this, but you can find many of the values on our list above even in popular genre books that often get belittled as "just" series fiction or beach reading. In both the Twilight saga and her novel *The Host*, it is quite clear that Stephenie Meyer feels strongly about what she sees as an eternal pair bond between men and women.

The Harry Potter series is often seen as an expression of the universal theme of good vanquishing evil, and indeed the books do center around that. But there is something more besides. The books are fiction; JK Rowling didn't write a memoir of her life. Still, one can clearly see what effects the loss of her mother to multiple sclerosis had on Rowling in what she wrote about the orphan Harry's grief for his parents, and in what the pivotal character of Dumbledore says about death.

Take some time to think about why you write—about why your writing is of worth to you.

Is it to entertain or educate, to exhort or express or maybe just escape? Is it, as Forster and the Ba'al Shem Tov suggested, to connect and heal?

If you're having a difficult time articulating your answer to this question, try writing it down in 25 words or so—in much the same way as you might summarize the heart of a story in order to pitch it to an agent, or share it with a friend.

And don't get discouraged if the answer still doesn't come clear to you all at once. I think most people discover their true reason for writing only gradually.

SPONTANEOUS COMBUSTION

When I first got the notion that I might want to write a book for kids, it started out merely as, "Oh, I can do better than this," when I was reading picture books to my son.

But over the years that mutated and evolved, a process that percolated so deep beneath the surface of my working mind that I wasn't consciously aware of it for a long time.

It was well after the publication of my first book that I—by accident—stumbled across the Ba'al Shem Tov quote. And it was as if this man from a different faith, different place, and different time had seen into my heart centuries ago. I had one of those "aha!" moments of recognition myself. I had found not my *raison d'être*, but my *raison d'écrire*.

I believe that's true for many other writers as well. Often it takes someone else—like an editor or reader—to tap us on the shoulder and awaken us to the writing purpose that was there all along, clear to everybody else's eyes but hidden from our own.

Whatever your answer, once you discover what your purpose is, you will be able to give your writing efforts the respect they deserve.

4
STOKE THE FIRE

Concrete things you can do

All this highfalutin talk may have rekindled your fire to write; I hope so, because that's sort of the point. But that flicker of inspiration has a tendency to fade when confronted with the light of day.

"Yeah, sure, I've got this noble calling to 'only connect' and help readers laugh and cry and transform their sorry lives," you may grumble. "That's fantastic, in theory. But I still don't know what the !#@$ I'm supposed to do every day to translate this into practice. And I've got to get this spreadsheet to my boss by 8 am tomorrow."

Fair enough. So how do you take your writing seriously? What specific actions can you take that will help you not only revive your passion to write, but sustain this creative fire over the long haul?

1. Put writing near the top of your priority list

For those of us who don't live as hermits in a cave somewhere, sustained by roots and berries, writing probably cannot be first on the list. Not only will we starve, but we may also drive away everyone we love if we ignore and neglect them. Still, writing needs to be pretty damn near the top.

And how do you demonstrate this commitment? By devoting yourself to writing. You may not have a lot of free time, but spend the time you do have on what you value: your writing.

Use your breaks at work to write rather than snack or gossip. John Grisham finished his first novel, *Time to Kill*, this way, drafting it in longhand on legal pads during court recesses. [Though I often wonder what his clients thought of his commitment to them.]

Get up early to write instead of sleeping in. The Georgia novelist Phil Williams did this, writing from 5:30 to 7:30 every morning before he went to work.

Spend your precious weekend or vacation time at a writer's seminar or conference.

Train for your craft with the same kind of intensity and discipline as an athlete training for the

Olympics. If novels are what you long to write, then read as many novels, and as many books and articles about how to write novels, as you can. Carry a notebook, tablet, or laptop with you everywhere and write as often as possible.

You get the idea. Basically I'm saying that if writing is truly your priority, you've got to do more than think about it: you've got to integrate it into the rhythms of your daily life. Strive to make it as much a part of you as breathing.

2. Write as regularly as you can

In my first draft, what I had here was that you should write every day. And if you can manage that, I still think it's a good idea. There is some alchemy that starts brewing in your brain when you write every day. You start to jones for your daily writing dose and feel incomplete—just plain wrong—when you miss it.

Maybe it's an endorphin thing like the fabled runner's high. I do know that when I have to miss my morning walk I get crabby. And when I am immersed in a writing project, such as this book, I also get cranky when something keeps me from working on it.

Right now, for example, I fled outside to sit under an umbrella in the rain because the sound of my husband and son elsewhere in the house was making it impossible to think. Two different TVs were blaring, and on top of that, every little cough, every slurp of soup stabbed like a needle straight through my eardrums to skewer the idea-generating portion of my brain.

But as addictive side effects go, crankiness is minor. If you have to be hooked on something, writing is a relatively safe thing to crave.

However, I'm not sure that writing every day is realistic for most writers—nor am I convinced that it's necessary.

Yes, Stephen King does it.

And I've read that some successful series writers are such slaves to a demanding publishing schedule that they have to write every day, too—even Christmas. If you ask me, if it gets to that point, it's time to kill off the main character in your series and retire on your royalties. You have to step outside your writing dungeon and live in order to have something to write about, you know.

But I'm getting sidetracked. Even if you can't write every single day of the week, I think you can keep your writing fires alive if you write on some kind of regular schedule.

Set yourself some kind of goal for the week rather than the day. It doesn't matter if your goal is how many hours you want to write, or how many words you want to produce. The Danish writer Isak Dinesen was only able to manage a half an hour a day during one bed-ridden year [her husband had given her syphilis]. But by writing regularly, she was still able to complete a novel in that year.

Ernest Hemingway didn't set himself a writing goal; he set a limit. When he completed 500 words, he stopped for the day, no matter what. He said that by stopping in the middle, rather than at the end of a scene, he found it easier to get started again the next day.

Whether you set a goal or a limit, in terms of time or word count, I'd suggest that you don't set them too high. If you tell yourself that you are going to write seven nights a week for five hours each night—and this after a full day's work and taking care of the kids and your ailing mother—you are setting yourself up to fail. And that failure will snuff out your desire to keep writing.

That's why I think that it's a better idea to set modest weekly writing goals rather than daily ones. Let's say that you promise yourself that will either write two hours a week on Saturday afternoon, or complete 500 words a week. Then if you get fired up and write three hours on Saturday, or are able to produce 1,000 words one week, you'll feel like a champion. Success like that is the best fuel to keep your writing fires alive.

3. Choose activities that nourish your writer's soul

To me, this is the single most important thing that we as writers need to do. When the rest of the world doesn't respect the time you spend writing, it gets harder and harder with each passing day to sustain your own sense of writerly purpose. So you need to seek out practices and activities that remind you of who you are, and who you want to continue to be.

This list is so long that I'm going to discuss it over two chapters.

3a. Hobnob with your fellow wizards

Writing is at heart a solitary pursuit. At that moment when you start reaching inside yourself to seize each word, each idea, each image, the cheese must stand alone. No one else can help; no one else can do this for you.

Thankfully, most writers thrive on solitude. Still, it is hard to be a church of one: to sustain your belief in what you do when you are the only practitioner you know. So if you can leave your sanctuary once in a while to connect with other writers, that will help you keep the faith.

Of course you can follow the oft-repeated advice to join a professional organization, get a critique group, or attend seminars and conferences. Going to a conference can be a real boon. Not only will you learn a great deal about both the craft and business of writing by doing this, it also feels a lot like Woodstock. Talk about revival!

But the buzz you get from hobnobbing with your fellow wizards at a conference eventually wears off. That's when you need to seek out one or two or three other people—whether that is down the street or across the globe—who share your passion for writing.

Sit together at a café or bistro for hours, or talk on the phone, workshopping each other's manuscripts-in-progress, or simply sharing what you're thinking and feeling and doing about writing. Email each other; videochat if you can.

But as our friend EM Forster said, "Only connect." If you can find just one other person who shares your belief in the joy and significance of writing, that will shore you up through the dark, empty times.

3b. Worship a literary hero

I started to use the word saint here, but writers are rarely saints, so it didn't fit. Find a writer whose work you admire, and then dig out the biographical details of his or her life. To me, that's inspiration. This works better if the writer is safely dead, in my opinion, but if you adore a living writer, you can use them for inspiration, too.

For this piece of advice, I'm less interested in what they wrote than how they wrote it, and what the circumstances of their lives were like while they were writing. When you read that Stephen King was working the night shift, living in a freezing trailer with his wife and babies, and typing on his knees while sitting on an overturned bucket in a closet before he sold *Carrie*, that gives you hope. If he could keep writing through times so tough, you can, too.

You may also want to copy out some of your favorite passages by your literary heroes, the ones that are so achingly good that you knew the first moment you read them that you wanted to create something that marvelous one day, too. Print them out, laminate them, and carry them in your wallet as a kind of writer's membership card.

I keep a collection of such quotes in a pocket-sized notebook, an old-fashioned practice called a commonplace book that was popular a couple hundred years ago. Trendy me.

One of the first quotes I wrote down in it is the opening paragraph from Shirley Jackson's *The Haunting of Hill House*, a book given to me by my father when I was just eleven.

> "No live organism can continue for long to exist under conditions of absolute reality; even larks and katydids are supposed, by some, to dream. Hill House, not sane, stood by itself against its hills, holding darkness within; it had stood so for eighty years and might stand for eighty more. Within, walls continued upright, bricks met neatly, floors were firm, and doors were sensibly shut; silence lay steadily against the wood and stone of Hill House, and whatever walked there, walked alone."

Whenever I need to remember what I hope to achieve with my writing, I re-read this. What favorite line or paragraph or page has this effect on you?

3c. Create a writing sanctuary

I don't care if it's a closet, an attic, basement, garage, or a tool shed in the back yard: you need a place to write. My dream is to have a writing studio in a tree house, although how I would be able to manage that with my bum knees is a real fantasy.

What I've got is a corner of the living room. Period. I don't have that Woolfian room of my own, just a portion of one in our charming but shall we say cozy 1880s-era Victorian cottage. [If by cozy you mean small.] My writing area is neither as roomy nor as quiet nor as private as I'd like, but over the years I've made it my sanctuary.

There is a quilt that I sewed hanging above my desk, along with an Edward Gorey cartoon, photos I've taken, old advertising posters of manual typewriters, and a Navajo sandpainting. There is also a file cabinet and a printer with Beanie babies nested in it, and a perilously-overcrowded bookcase. My desk is the same one I've used since I was ten, and I've tried every space-maximizing strategy I can find to use every inch so it can fit my laptop, iPad mini, and all my other writing paraphernalia.

It's not much, but it's mine. No matter how tiny or humble your writing area is, take whatever measures you can to make it yours as well. Especially if, like me, you have to make do with part of a room that is used by others for other purposes, it's important to do whatever you can to set it aside, to mark it as your writing territory.

That's why I've gone to such pains to fill my little writing nook with things that have meaning to me, that I've created, that define it as my space. You should do the same. Even if all you have is a TV tray that you have to stash behind the couch when company comes, the mere fact that your laptop [or notebook and pens] lives on that tray sets it apart as your writing space.

I know that many members of our writing tribe live in circumstances where solitude is almost impossible to get—even in the bathroom. In that case, you may have to resort to extreme measures. I often write outside at a picnic table under pecan trees when noise or activity invade my writing alcove; and I've read about authors who have used their cars as their mobile writing studios.

If all else fails, your lap and your notebook may have to be your office. In that case, try this. Get a set of headphones and use them to block out the sound around you.

Whatever you have to do, and wherever you can claim it, you need to mark out a writing space. There is something about the psychology of routine that helps you make the transition to writing more readily if you habitually do it in one place.

And there is another reason I think creating a space specifically for your writing is so important. The religious scholar Mircea Eliade talks about the distinction all religions make between regular space and sacred space.

There is a reason people leave their homes and go to special buildings to worship. There is a reason they lavish so much of their time and resources to construct these buildings and make them beautiful. It is because they believe they are making a home for the divine, and setting that place apart as holy.

Your writing sanctuary may not be sacred. But having a place, however small, that you think of as separate and different from all the other space in your home, can be another thing you can do to take yourself seriously as a writer.

3d. Escape your space occasionally and write somewhere different

I know this sounds like a contradiction of what I just said above, but writing rules are a lot like the Pirate's Code: more like guidelines really. The cafés so beloved of writing guru Natalie Goldberg in her book *Writing Down the Bones* may actually be good for you, cognitive science now says. There is something about a low level of distraction in the background that helps you focus better; perhaps because you have to work a little harder to keep that focus.

This only works, however, if there isn't too much noise or distraction in the background. For example, I find the background music at most Starbucks stores too loud and intrusive, but sometimes I can get work done there. My local coffee shop isn't private enough either. I live in a small town and people will keep stopping by my table to say hello, blast them!

But if you can find a public space that strikes a happy medium between a circus and a monastery, then by all means, write there. Just remember to buy something every hour or so. The restaurant needs to pay the rent, too.

Another way to escape your usual writing space is to travel. It is a cliché that we travel to find ourselves, but I do think that travel can be enriching for a writer. I love the poet Kathleen Norris' book *Dakota: A Spiritual Geography;* and I agree that the place a writer lives can shape and nourish his or her work.

But you don't have to live somewhere for it to feed your writing. I believe that a change of scene can cause an explosion of creativity, so take advantage of that. Be sure to take your laptop or notebook or tablet wherever you go.

I'm glad I did that. After years of trying, I finally discovered the true setting of my first novel, *Cheshire Moon*, when I was on a family vacation in Islesboro, Maine. I fell in love with the island and did a lot of research when I was supposed to be spending time with my family. [My nephew once drew up an award for me: "The Hardest Worker on Vacation." Oops.]

Then I transformed Islesboro into the fictional island of Summerhaven, and ended up writing what became the first few chapters of my novel during the two weeks I was there.

3e. Create a writing time

I've already written about this in item 2 above, but let me add something here. One of the things that many writers have found—if they retired, found a sugar daddy/mama, or were otherwise fortunate enough not to need a day job to survive—is that the more free time they had, the harder it was to write. Paradoxically, it is often when you have only a limited time for your writing that your creativity and productivity blossom.

I'm not sure what kind of reverse psychology may be at work here, but I know that in my own experience, it is often when I'm swamped with deadlines from my "other" work—teaching, freelance editing, educational work-for-hire—that I find that my usual fiction-writing pace suddenly shifts from glacial to volcanic. In other words, I'm suddenly able to write thousands of words instead of hundreds of words in a writing session—and I'm driven to do it, just when I've got zero time.

So perhaps you should be thankful for that sense that you have to wrestle your schedule for every minute of writing time. The battle itself may make the time so precious to you that you are able to get more done.

Many writers also say that inspiration strikes not as a lightning bolt from above, but arises from ground that they've prepared by constantly tilling it. In other words, if you aren't writing regularly, you won't be around to welcome her when the Muse finally does decide to drop by.

I'm not sure about that. For one thing, I've read about plenty of productive writers who claim that they only write when they're inspired; that if they try to force themselves to write, all they produce is dreck.

Joseph Conrad, author of *Heart of Darkness*, was one of these tortured writers. In a letter to a friend, Conrad wrote:

"I sit down religiously every morning. I sit down for eight hours every day—and the sitting down is all. In the course of that working day of eight hours I write three sentences which I erase before leaving the table in despair. Sometimes it takes all my resolution and power of self-control to refrain from butting my head against the wall. I want to howl and foam at the mouth but I daren't do it for fear of waking the baby and alarming my wife."

Enough said.

I've experienced both sides of this "which comes first, the work or the inspiration" conundrum. There have been times when I've been able to squeeze out a workable idea when I was completely dry by forcing myself to sit down and brainstorm one. Most of the time, however, that hasn't worked for me.

That's one reason why I'm so compulsive about carrying notebooks around with me everywhere—so I can capture those evanescent soap-bubbles of inspiration right away, before they *pop!* in a passing whisper of air and I lose them forever.

On the other hand, I do find that the more I write, the more likely it is that I will be able to develop the ideas I already have into stories that live and breathe. One idea tends to grow another, in a creative chain reaction that is like those time-lapse videos of lattices exploding inside a crystal. That perpetual motion machine of ideas wouldn't happen if I weren't writing, and writing a lot.

But sometimes my most fertile ideas have often come to me when I wasn't writing at all. I've written about this "cross-training" effect on my website, but I've found that I periodically need to get up from my keyboard, go outside, and do something else.

Whether that is going for a walk, washing dishes, watching movies, knitting, playing my dulcimer, or going for a long drive, it is often when I stop writing for a time that ideas work themselves loose from my subconscious and pop into my mind.

SPONTANEOUS COMBUSTION

The American playwright Edward Albee had a vivid way of describing this pre-writing activity.

> "It's like a dog—the way a dog before it craps wanders around in circles....It's like that, figuratively circling the typewriter."

Sometimes it take a lot of circling before you can end a bout of creative constipation.

After a long period of struggle, my first novel finally came together for me one day while I was driving home from an errand, idly listening to the radio. All of a sudden I heard a voice, and not the usual inner narrator either— you know, the one who is always droning on, day in and day out.

This voice sounded like something completely Other, perched on my shoulder and whispering in my ear. [It's okay when writers hear voices; it doesn't mean we're insane. Really.]

The voice murmured to me that my main character was deaf. That came as a complete revelation to me. I had no idea that she might be deaf, but the minute I realized that, the book that I had spent many sterile years trying to write came together for me. I parked the car on the shoulder of the road, took out a notebook, and sketched the outline for the entire novel in about fifteen minutes.

That's why I'm not sure that you have to be constantly writing in order to generate inspiration. It does help, but I think the real key is finding the perfect balance. Spend *enough* time writing—and enough time living with your writing ideas even when you aren't at your desk—that the embers of inspiration are always smoldering.

One thing that doesn't work for me, at least not in my fiction writing, is trying to trick myself into writing by imposing deadlines on myself. Now if I have an external deadline, one set by an editor somewhere waiting for me to finish a project, I will not rest—literally, I won't sleep—until I finish. Early. I can't stand to be late, and to me, being on time feels almost like being late. So I make sure I've got every last comma in place well in advance of my deadline.

However, if I try to impose some deadline on myself—say, to finish that chapter by Thursday—it won't work. I can't fool myself; I know the worst thing that's going to happen if I miss the deadline is that…well, I'll miss the deadline. I'm not a scary enough boss for myself, I guess.

But if the deadline trick works for you, then use it.

5
MORE FUEL

Writing rituals and auxiliary brains

The tips I gave in the previous chapter for how you can take your writing seriously were all fairly practical. The suggestions in this chapter are bit, well...less practical, especially the first one about writing rituals.

Besides, the last chapter was getting too long. I needed to give you guys a break.

3f. Create a writing ritual

A writing ritual doesn't have to be something flaky or New Age-y. If you prefer, you can think of this more as warm-up exercises, like athletes do to limber up before they start training in earnest.

Whatever you call it, and whatever you choose to do for your writing ritual, I think such rituals are useful in order to help you make the transition from ordinary time to writing time.

If this sounds familiar, it is; it's an extension of Mircea Eliade's concept of sacred space. If churches and temples and mosques help believers feel that they have entered a space that is reserved for the holy, then rituals are the counterpart in time and action.

Lighting candles, burning incense, uttering chants or prayers, kneeling, bowing, washing hands and feet—the repertoire of ritual actions goes on. And they are all designed to create the sense that something different, something wondrous, something special is about to happen. The person is about to leave ordinary time and enter into a kind of eternity.

You can do something similar to help you feel, when you sit down to write, that you too are stepping into the realm of the extraordinary. And you don't have to use candles and incense either, not unless you want to.

For example, the Broadway choreographer Twyla Tharp in her book *The Creative Habit* writes about a whole host of things she does to keep her in a creative mindset every day. She's a dancer, not a writer, so her rituals are specific to her art.

One thing she does every day before she enters the studio is eat an egg white omelet and go through a set routine of stretches. She sees this as more than nutrition and exercise; she sees them as rituals that helps ease her into a mindset where she can be open and creative.

Writing rituals can be very simple. I once heard the YA writer Han Nolan say that she simply drank a glass of water and said a little prayer each day when she came to her computer.

For me walking is the way I shift from the ordinary world to my own private writing world. I am convinced people in the town where I live think of me as the Mad Walker. Once I start walking, I am gone. I am thinking about my characters, or my freelance client's characters: who they are and what they want and what messes they are getting themselves into and out of.

I don't see people waving to me from their cars. I'm aware of where I am, enough not to stumble and fall on my face. But even though I'm walking down the sidewalk and past the old Victorian homes of my town, that's not where I am: not mentally. I am somewhere else. I'm not sure where I go actually, but it feels like some place outside time—like the Wood Between the Worlds in CS Lewis' *The Magician's Nephew*.

SPONTANEOUS COMBUSTION

I start each writing day with a two-mile walk. Then when I return home, I make tea. And I don't just dump a tea bag in a chipped mug and nuke it in the microwave either.

I've gone to a lot of effort to assemble the ingredients for a proper English tea. I've haunted eBay and collected earthenware teapots and transferware tea cups. I buy loose tea in several varieties from a British importer, and I've even knitted several tea cozies, which like Hermione's in Harry Potter, work equally well as hats.

I bring a pot of freshly-drawn water to a boil, swish a little in the teapot to warm it up, then add the leaves to a strainer and infuse them with the hot water. The agony of the leaves, it's called, that moment when the tea leaves suddenly unfurl in the boiling bath. Maybe that's my writer's sacrifice: that the leaves should suffer agony so I don't when I begin to write.

When the tea is steeped and strained, I pour it into a cup. That slightly bitter, slightly astringent first sip hits me like some kind of word-inducing drug. In that moment, I can feel something shift inside me. I've made one more step away from the ordinary world to the story world I'm about to create.

Maybe this whole English tea ritual works for me because I adore British writers such as Jane Austen, CS Lewis, JRR Tolkien, Agatha Christie, Barbara Pym, Dorothy Sayers, and so many others. Maybe when I make my tea the way the characters in their novels made theirs, I am sucked into the World of Writing. I don't know. Rituals don't bear too much analysis.

All I know is that it's what I do. Though I do think that the amount of work I invested in creating the ritual, gathering teapots and cups and knitting tea-hats, has something to do with why it works for me. That commitment of time and energy charged the ritual, the way you charge a battery, so it could fuel the transformation from regular time to writing time.

Now go play! See what you can do that helps you set your work as a writer apart as something special and valuable.

Here is a list of possible ideas for rituals with which you might inaugurate your writing day.

🍂 Say a prayer or chant

🍂 Light a candle, perhaps one in a scent that soothes or energizes you

🍂 Make up your own coffee ritual

🍂 Read a quote from one of your favorite authors about writing, a passage of a favorite book, or perhaps a poem

🍂 Do a stretching exercise such as the sun salute from yoga

🍂 Play a favorite song or piece of music*

[*Many writers talk about finding specific songs that inspire them when writing certain scenes, or when trying to get into the heads of individual characters. Stephenie Meyer of Twilight fame has quite famously published her "soundtrack" for those books on her website.]

3g. Find your auxiliary brain

Simply put, your auxiliary brain is whatever tool you use to write. Writers wax rhapsodic about their particular choices, claiming that the nature and quality of what they write is intimately affected by whether they write it longhand, on a typewriter, or on a computer. I've even seen claims that writing with a fountain pen produces more thoughtful, flowing sentences that does writing with a ballpoint!

Experiment and find what meshes best with the way you write. I've tried them all, even ballpoint versus fountain pen. I went through a phase of tapping out my rough drafts on a collection of vintage manual typewriters from the 30s and 40s.

I must admit, there is something about the resistance of the keys beneath your fingers, the sound of the bell at the end of the line, the image of the words appearing the instant you type them—even the musty, oily smell of the old machines—that made me feel like I was channeling the spirit of Raymond Chandler.

It doesn't matter what you end up using. What does matter is that whatever writing tool you use comes to feel so natural that it no longer stands in the way of what you want to say— when it even seems to anticipate what you want to write the moment that you think it. That's when a writing tool becomes your auxiliary brain.

What I'm talking about here is a concept popularized by philosopher Andy Clark in his book on cognitive science, *Natural-Born Cyborgs*. Clark says that when you use a tool to help you manage information, it becomes an extension of your brain. (My apologies to Clark and to his former student, my son Evan, for the gross over-simplification.)

It may take you a while to find the writing tool that becomes so much a part of you that merely sitting down to use it activates the "on-switch" in your imagination. It took me several years of auditioning and discarding tools until I finally found the one that fused with me.

My Macbook Air is my auxiliary brain. I never go anywhere without it. My life is on it. Everything I've ever written, or tried to write, or thought about writing, or wrote and hated, is on there. To me, nothing is real until I write it down on my Air. It truly feels as if the axons and dendrites of my central nervous system have a direct connection with the computer.

But if you don't like your computer, and it doesn't like you, then it's not your auxiliary brain. Find the tool that is, even if that means you're writing with pencil stubs on cocktail napkins.

I don't use napkins, but I still do some of my writing—especially during the brainstorming and planning parts of a project—by hand, on paper. As attached as I am to my Macbook Air, I am also addicted to pocket-sized notebooks.

Some people stockpile toilet paper; I stockpile blank notebooks. I have them in every color of the spectrum, and I strew them everywhere. There are at least two in my purse, one on my bedside table, one in the glove compartment of my car, and a stack of them at my desk. Yes, I write in my notebooks at the same time as I write on my Air; both feel necessary to me.

I keep a separate notebook for each novel that I'm working on. And don't forget that commonplace book I mentioned in chapter 4.

So I suppose you could say that I have a two-lobed auxiliary brain: half-digital, half-paper.

The only way you can find your auxiliary brain is to try them all, to find out which tool becomes part of you.

🌶 Will you be like most writers today, and use a desktop or laptop computer?

🌶 Will you use a tablet computer or even a smartphone [with or without an external keyboard]?

🌶 Will you be like the Nobel Prize laureate Toni Morrison, who wrote *Beloved* in longhand on paper?

🌶 Will you be like Cormac McCarthy, Don DeLillo, David McCullough, P.J. O'Rourke, and Brian Jacques, all of whom write on manual typewriters?

🌶 Maybe you won't write your books at all— you'll dictate them!

3h. Read the scripture (but know when to stop)

Reading, and reading a lot, is something I already alluded to in the last chapter. But it bears repeating, because here I am speaking of something a bit more targeted. Read books by other writers about how they write. Go to conferences and seminars and collect stories told by the speakers of how they write. Read articles about writing.

What you are trying to do with all this study of the writing scripture is feed your soul, absorbing nutrients from this constant flood of advice, encouragement, exhortation, and information, as if by osmosis. I don't care if you promptly forget the specific advice you read or hear in all this study, because that's not the point. When you are trying to remind yourself that what you are doing is worthwhile, the details aren't all that important. All you want to do is immerse yourself in the stream, to soak it all in.

But a word of caution here. You can overdo this, getting all wrinkled and prune-y from too long a submersion. So you need to know when it's time to withdraw: to stop all this reading so you can climb back inside your own head and write what only you know.

For two chapters, I've sketched some activities that you can cultivate in order to help you take writing seriously, to weave it into the texture of your life. Take what works for you and discard the rest. Explore and find other things I haven't mentioned that help you.

It comes down to is this. If you truly value your writing—if you want to live as a writer rather than just dream of being one—then the way to do that is by devoting your personal resources to it: time, money, physical energy, and creative juices.

Why not start now?

6

CONVERTING THE DEMONS OF DOUBT

Writer's malaise: doubt, fear, and anxiety

Midway in the journey of our life
I came to myself in a dark wood,
For the straight way was lost.
[Translation by Robert and Jean Hollander]

At some point in his or her career, every writer stumbles off the path. As I say on the home page of my website, these opening lines of Dante's *Divine Comedy* have special relevance for writers. We all get lost. It may be in the middle of a novel, when we suddenly stop being able to see what happens next with our characters, or we get waylaid on a plot detour that bogs us down in quicksand at the end. Or it may be in the middle of the morning, when all of a sudden our desk is the last place we want to be.

Call it the long dark night of the writer's soul; call it, as I do, getting lost in the Dantean dark wood. It doesn't matter. I don't mean to scare you, but if you are reading this book you have probably already experienced it anyway. So let me just say it. Sooner or later, the fickle Muse *will* desert you; it's what she does.

The good news, however, is that she will return. That's what she does, too. But when you are lost and alone in the grim woods, you won't believe that. So how do you get through these unavoidable periods of writerly despair?

Some don't. That's the reality of the writing life. The stereotype of the starving, struggling, desperate, despondent writer who turns to drink, drugs, sex, or suicide is a stereotype for a reason.

Look at Kay Redfield Jamison's book *Touched With Fire*. A psychiatrist, manic-depressive [her preferred term for the syndrome most like to call bipolar disorder] and writer herself, Jamison's book states that the prevalence of depression is higher in writers than among the general population.

Whether people who battle depression and anxiety are more prone to write, or whether writers are more prone to depression and anxiety, is a chicken-and-egg problem whose solution is beside the point for those who are living through it.

But I'm not talking about the clinical diagnosis of depression; that is beyond my expertise. What I'm talking about here are the periods of doubt, fear, and anxiety that seem to dog writers. Remember our mantra?

> Take your writing seriously,
> because nobody else will.

Doubt and fear and anxiety are huge obstacles to doing that. That's why I'm devoting a chapter to them.

Even though I was already a published writer when I started my first YA novel, having worked for many years as a newspaper reporter and editor, I kept my "fiction addiction" secret. I told no one that I was working on a book, not for the thirteen long years it took me to finally finish *Cheshire Moon*. Why did it take so long? And why did I keep it a secret?

Because deep down inside, I was sure I'd fail. The only part of me that seemed certain of anything was absolutely convinced that I was a lousy writer with a lame story and that I would never, never, *never* get published. The pain and humiliation of failure would be easier to bear, I felt, if I was the only one who knew about it.

My second YA novel, *The Door in the Lake*, took me only thirteen months to write, and everybody knew I was working on it. Happy ending, right?

Not so fast.

Though I went on to build a steady career as a writer, leaving the security of the newspaper to publish more articles and books—and also to teach, speak, and eventually become a book editor myself—in some ways I've regressed. After my publisher turned down my third novel manuscript, saying it was the best writing I'd ever done but he didn't feel it was marketable, I tanked.

Technically, I wasn't blocked. I was still able to write, publishing both fiction and non-fiction in the education market. But something was missing. I had lost my nerve. I finished a fourth book of fiction for kids, but was too afraid to show it to my publisher.

I still have the manuscript; I never delete anything I write. But entropy is probably taking care of that for me. As I write this, both my third and fourth books are probably disappearing day by day from my hard drive, bit by de-magnetized bit.

I started a fifth novel for kids, rewriting it three times but never getting to the end. I got a brainstorm for an adult novel somewhere in there, too.

The majority of my time was spent, not writing my own books, but helping thousands of other people writer theirs. And I love that work. When one of my students gets published, I am as proud and overjoyed as if I'd done it myself. It is a gift to be able to shepherd someone along the often perilous path from getting an idea to shaping it into a book.

Still, as much as I love editing, it was my own stories I wanted to tell. And I didn't seem to be able to do that.

In working with students and book clients, they have shared similar experiences with me. They too go through long periods not of writer's block, but of doubt, fear, and despair. They can still write, at times, but it is almost a punishment. Some days they are able to drag themselves to their desks and force themselves to crank out a sentence, a paragraph, a page. But more often or not, the words they manage to set down on the page seem parched and lifeless to them.

Not surprisingly, with "rewards" like this for their efforts, they find it harder and harder to make themselves sit down at their desks in the first place. Any excuse will do: unclogging the toilet, or spending their free afternoon at the rest home listening to their great-uncle rant about the decline of Western civilization.

A lot has been written about the twin problems of both procrastination and writer's block, so I'm not going to attempt to duplicate that here. In any case, I'm not sure that either of those labels really applies to the experience I'm trying rather ineptly to describe. Writers can still write, and they still believe that they want to write. Yet they dread the very thing they long for: either that, or their dream of writing paradoxically leaves them cold.

They have lost their passion, their zest.

The more I heard these stories from my students, and the longer I experienced it myself, the more I came to believe that this wasn't writer's block *per se*, and it wasn't true procrastination either.

Maybe writer's malaise would be a better word for it. But whatever you call it, doubt and fear are at the heart of it.

I don't have any pat answers as to how you can exorcise these writer's demons. No two writers are alike—and the specific form that doubt and fear take can vary from one period to another in the same writer's life. So there is no single sure-fire technique that can help.

However, I would recommend two books: *The Courage to Write*, by Ralph Keyes; and Anne Lamott's *Bird by Bird*.

Keyes' book is less well-known, and a bit more analytic in tone, but don't let that put you off. It is a comprehensive and compassionate study of the role that anxiety plays in writing, based both on Keyes' thirty years of teaching and on the experience of numerous writers, famous and not-so-famous. Far from depressing you, I think Keyes' book will give you back your writing heart.

Whereas Lamott's book will make you laugh. And when you are lost in the woods, laughter is an excellent way to tame your fears. Second, try these two approaches.

Wait it out

Try to remember that doubt comes in cycles. When the manuscript you've written seems so awful today that you not only want to burn it, you also want to back your car over the computer on which you wrote it, don't! Instead, wait. In a few days or a few weeks, those same words will seem like the best lines ever written. Not that you should trust that euphoria either, but the point is that the judgments you make about your work—about the worth of your writing— are going to fluctuate.

Doubt waxes and wanes, just like the phases of the lunatic moon. And as the character Fenoglio says in Cornelia Funke's *Inkspell*, "All writers are lunatics." He should know; he is a writer himself. And so are you.

So stand your ground. Wait it out.

Sometimes in order to do this it helps to keep an image in your head, so here is one I borrowed from what I've read about various forms of meditation. [I've tried meditation and I'm lousy at it, so don't take anything I say on that subject as authoritative.]

It starts with understanding the nature of waves. Waves only agitate the surface of the ocean; the water at the bottom stays calm. So when you start to get agitated by doubts and fears, imagine yourself as a rock on the smooth, untroubled bottom of the sea. Even when a tidal wave of doubt is rushing straight at you try, as much as you are able, to let gravity hold you firmly on the bottom while the doubt swirls over your head—and ultimately past you.

In other words, try to avoid letting the tide of emotion carry you away. Stand aside from yourself for a moment and say, "Yep, here it comes: that tsunami of doubt is back. But it's an outside force, not part of me. This too shall pass."

This is where any writing habits you've cultivated—writing space, writing time, writing wizards, writing heroes, a writing ritual—can help. The more of those you have, and the more time you've poured into building and strengthening them, the greater the force of writing gravity there will be. This is what will help anchor you in place while the undertow of doubt is threatening to drag you out to sea.

And remember: doubt is a big fat liar. When it tells you that you are the worst writer who ever lived, and that everything you've written is dreck, don't believe it. Plug your ears if you have to, but don't listen.

Channel your fear

Or you can try to co-opt the doubt. What I mean by that is that you steal its energy and use it for something else, something more constructive—like your writing.

Divert, convert, and subvert: that's what you want to do.

This works better if the problem you are facing is anxiety, not doubt. Doubt tends to have negative energy; like the Dementors in JK Rowling's Harry Potter books, doubt sucks all hope and happiness and certainty right out of you.

But I think in most cases what we call writer's block is actually fear or anxiety masquerading as doubt. Behind the doubt is the fear that we aren't good enough, our writing isn't good enough, our stories aren't worth telling.

And even if we do manage to slay those particular dementors of doubt, then we might still fear that even if our stories are worth telling, and even if we do have the skills to tell them, that maybe we will reveal too much of ourselves in the process. That maybe we will let ourselves be known. And that makes us vulnerable.

I believe that fear is the real power behind doubt. But both fear and its cousin anxiety have a kind of hectic, festering energy. They prickle under our skin and make us twitchy, or rankle in our bowels and make us restless, uneasy. We don't sit still when we're anxious; we pace.

That's the energy you can appropriate. Like Prometheus stealing fire, we writers need to steal the heat and light that hides within fear and use it for creation, not destruction: to create something so it won't destroy us.

OK, that all sounds lovely and makes a great metaphor, but what the !@#$! does it mean in practical terms? The best way I can illustrate it is to share my own experience.

I went through a year where everything seemed to go wrong. My 130-year-old house, which I love—well, most of the time—needed a new porch, a new roof, a new water heater, and a new dryer. [OK, so it didn't need the dryer; I did.]

My husband wrecked our old car and when the insurance declared it a total loss, we had to buy a new car—the week before I was scheduled for surgery to relieve compression on the spinal cord in my neck.

The idea that someone would be using bone saws and drills within millimeters of my spinal cord was a nightmare. But I was having bizarre neurologic symptoms, like falling over for no reason, and being unable to type. And without this surgery that scared me witless, those symptoms might be permanent, or even get worse. So I agreed to have it.

Then as I was recovering from the surgery, the doctors told us that my father would die within days from renal failure. Three days stretched into three weeks, and I made three 1300-mile round trips to be with him and my family, and to say good-bye. It was an excruciating time.

Writing? Forget about it. I was completely stalled, both on Kids Novel #5 and on that adult novel that I'd been toying with for a couple of years. Though at one time I had felt a deep kinship with the protagonists of both books, now I felt so disconnected from them that they might as well have been living on the dark side of the moon. Neither one of them was talking to me. And I was so afraid that I had lost them forever that I didn't dare read the partially-written manuscripts.

You're done

they would tell me.

You're finished as a writer.

As if all this weren't enough, two weeks after my father died, our second car also decided to give up the ghost. It had to be replaced, too.

At this point, I hadn't been able to do as much teaching and editing work as I was used to for several months. My income had dried to a trickle. But I had to have a car, so what else could I do? With a crushing sense of dread, I took on a monthly payment.

For me, that was the final straw. The unlikely combination of a car payment and my father's death tipped me over the edge.

I woke up one morning, and though in one sense the worst had already happened—my dad was gone—I couldn't shake the feeling; no, the certainty, the absolute conviction—that something even worse was about to happen, no matter what I did. Every minute of every day felt like a catastrophe just about to pounce, and I was in full panic mode all the time, my muscles clenching, my heart constantly stuttering in my chest.

It took about two weeks of this before I finally turned around and named it. By that I mean that I recognized that what I was feeling was probably not a realistic reflection of the way things were, but rather fear, anxiety—a weird manifestation of grief from a year's worth of loss and stress.

My response? Though I can't say I planned it, I woke up every day and channeled that anxiety into action. All of a sudden I decided I needed to make a renewed commitment to myself as a writer.

I set up the website that I'd sworn for years that I would never do—and though initially it felt like a lot of work and confusion for nothing, after a day or two I got completely caught up in the creative joy of designing and building it. I was especially excited by writing a series of articles to add substance to the site. I love teaching, and this enabled me to do that.

I renewed my dormant membership in SCBWI, the professional organization of children's writers, and set up a profile there. I polished my resume and sent it out to a series of educational publishers. One of the things I do to keep the wolf from the door is work-for-hire for such publishers, but I hadn't really pursued that aggressively for some time.

I got back in touch with writer-friends whom I hadn't contacted in a few years, and was rewarded with an outpouring of heartfelt responses. It did me such good to be hobnobbing with my fellow wizards again.

Converting the Demons of Doubt

After all this, one night I dropped down in a chair, intending to vege out with a night of TV. Instead, I was suddenly inspired to write an article for a magazine devoted to children's writing. I got the idea at 8 pm, researched it on my trusty auxiliary brain, and finished the first draft by midnight. I let it sit overnight [a revision practice I recommend to all writers], then rewrote it the next morning and sent it off to an editor I'd worked with in the past.

The more I wrote, the more writing ideas I got. This kind of cross-fertilization is one of the most welcome side effects of spontaneous combustion. I started a list of ideas for articles for my website. I'd be out walking, or curling up under a blanket after my nightly shower, or sitting down with that ritual cup of tea, and more ideas kept percolating out of that writhing mass of fear and anxiety inside me.

And the more seriously I took those ideas, actually sitting down to develop them in writing, the less power the fear had over me.

The anxiety was still there; I hadn't fully banished that. But I had dug a new channel for it, diverting and taming its potentially destructive force and turning it into a wellspring of writing. It was this same wellspring of writerly energy that enabled me to find the courage to take a second look at two book projects—a novel for kids and a novel for adults— that I had shelved years ago, believing them to be unworkable, worthless.

You should never listen to those demons whispering in your ear. When I did look at the manuscripts, I realized that they both had promise. I had to choose one though, so I resumed working on the middle grade novel.

And while I was doing that, I got the brainstorm for this book.

If this sounds like amateur therapy, that is not my intent. All I can say is that when you are afflicted with the doubt that seems to torture and plague all writers at some point in their lives, perhaps one of these approaches will help see you through it.

❧ Let the doubt flood past you, recognizing it for what it is: a temporary distraction that says nothing about your talent or worth as a writer.
❧ Drain the destructive energy from fear by turning that energy into fuel for your writing.

And by so doing, you will find your way back onto the writing path.

7
SWITCH HIT

Give the Muse a taste
of her own medicine

The Muse wasn't speaking to me when I got to my desk this morning. "Typical!" I said. "Set me ablaze with this book about spontaneous combustion, then show up with a fire extinguisher."

For the past seventeen days, words, sentences, pages, and whole chapters have flowed out of me, almost without effort. But today I got stuck on three paragraphs I was trying to revise. Nothing I did would pry the right words loose. I went for my ritual walk, even though the a cold east wind was blowing rain down my neck. I drank my ritual tea. I sat in my writing sanctuary at the appointed writing time and re-read my quote from the Ba'al Shem Tov.

Still nothing.

But this isn't my first dance with the Muse. I know her mercurial ways, and after decades of writing, I've learned a few tricks. So I decided to give her a taste of her own medicine.

I stopped trying.

This flies in the face of the advice I've always read about gritting your teeth, hunkering down, and plowing your way through a block, whether it's large or small. "Stay at your desk," we're told. "Keep writing, no matter what."

But I'm going to suggest that when your words dry up, stop.

Stop pleading and whining and begging, promising anything to the Muse if she will only come back and help. In my experience, this just makes her snicker and stay away even longer.

So turn your back on her for a change; see how she likes it.

This is what I call switch hitting. If the words won't come, then stop trying to make them. Do something entirely different for a while instead.

Abandon your writing post

Go to the movies or the golf course. Mow your lawn or spend the day on the beach with your best friends. If you have the time and money, go for a cruise to the Antarctic.

Admittedly, this is the riskiest approach. The farther you get from your writing space, and the more of your writing time you spend doing something else, the greater the danger that you may be gone so long that the Muse will forget all about you and find some new writer to torment…er, I mean, grace with her presence.

But some times this "nuclear option" does the trick; it blasts you out of your block. I think it works because once you've saturated yourself long enough with a story or idea, it permeates every level of your mind, from the attic of your conscious, working brain all the way down to the sub-basement. And you know how that is. It's when you forget about all the things that you've squirreled away in your basement that they start to grow stuff.

Granted, the kind of stuff that grows in your literal basement—mold, mildew, and other unspeakable new life forms—isn't exactly welcome. But we're talking about a metaphorical basement. And the ideas in your stories need some time in the dark and damp in order to germinate.

SPONTANEOUS COMBUSTION

Try a different form of creativity

I've written about this before, both in this book and on my website, so I won't belabor the point. But writing is a verbal art, so try one of the non-verbal forms of creativity for a change. Paint, sculpt, throw pots. Tune up the guitar that's been languishing in your closet since you left college and see if your fingers still remember those chords. Draw the curtains so you don't scare the neighbors, put on some music, and dance.

Without getting into the debate about how accurate the left brain/right brain theories of mental function are, cognitive science does tell us that when we do new things, we create new neural connections between various areas of our brains. I believe that when we try creative pursuits in other modalities such as music, art, or dance, we may stimulate the writing portion of our brains as well. This can be just what we need to ease our way out of a block.

Write something different

This is perhaps the safest and best approach. Instead of giving up on your writing time all together when you are blocked, try a different form of writing.

I do this all the time. I write fiction and non-fiction, both for adults and for children. So when I get blocked on an adult non-fiction project, as I did this morning, I set it aside and work on something for kids instead. That's when it's good to have a few different projects going on at once.

Or you can switch hit by shifting from one stage of the writing process to another. When you are just starting a new story or book, you tend to brainstorm and plan and organize. That's one stage. Then there is the wondrous stage when you pour your ideas out in the rough first draft, not yet worried about what your editor, agent, critique group, sister, or boyfriend may think about it. That's the writing stage. Then there are the umpteen passes you make through a manuscript to polish and perfect it. That's the revision stage.

If I'm stuck during revision, as I was this morning, then I may change gears and work on the first draft of another section of the same manuscript; or I may brainstorm an entirely new project.

Some writers, such as Stephen King, actually plan their writing days to routinely switch hit. King says he works on new material during the morning, and revises older projects in the afternoon.

I'm not a poet, but if you write both poetry and prose, this is another way you can switch hit. If the prose you're cranking out for a scene in your novel is wooden, stop trying to force it. For a while at least, go back to one of your poems.

This kind of switch hitting tends to shake up the Muse. She's a bit of a drama queen; she doesn't like it when you take the spotlight off her. She's willing to make some concessions in order to get you back.

What can I say? It worked for me this morning. Not only did I get a student manuscript edited, and that pesky paragraph rewritten, I got this whole new chapter as well.

The Muse is speaking to me again.

8
FAKING IT

Pretend you're a writer

I had finished both the first draft and the revision of this book when something suggested, in a giggly sort of whisper, that I add this chapter. [As I told you before, it's normal for writers to hear voices. You believe me, right?]

The idea was so goofy that I wasn't sure whether to listen to this particular voice or not, but here goes.

When you have trouble either believing in your writing, or in yourself as a writer, fake it. Remember when you were a kid and you would play, "Let's pretend?" That's what I'm talking about.

People are always advising aspiring or blocked writers, "Just do it," or some version of that tough-love advice. Quit your belly-aching, plunk your butt down, and just write already, they say.

The problem is, such brute force techniques don't work. The prescription is the same as the disease. If you were able to make yourself sit down and write, you wouldn't have turned to them for advice in the first place. It's like a doctor prescribing a daily walk to a paralyzed person. "Just walk already." If only they could.

That's why I think that sometimes it may help to kick start your creative efforts if you stop trying to convince yourself that you're a serious writer. I know that goes against everything I've written thus far, but hear me out.

If you feel ridiculous when you try to write, like some kind of fraud, don't deny it. Accept it. Embrace it even. Shout it out loud. "Yep, I'm a fraud. I'm only pretending to be a real writer."

And then get busy pretending. If you feel like you're only play-acting when you think of yourself as a writer, then throw yourself into the role as if you were an actor hoping to win an Academy Award for your performance.

🖤 Gather your props and costume.

   If you're a hard-boiled mystery writer, get your fedora, Royal typewriter, and a bottle of cheap whiskey.

If you're a romance writer, get your feather boa, your pink laptop, and a pitcher of peach bellinis.

If you're a true crime writer, strap on your camera and digital recorder, and get ready to buy some boilermakers to pry secrets out of witnesses down at the local pool hall.

Clearly I'm indulging in hyperbole here. But if you're going to pretend to be a writer, do it right. At the very least, get your computer or your typewriter or your legal pad and set it out on your desk.

❦ Run your lines.

Face your mirror and practice saying, "I'm a writer" out loud; or, "Sorry, I can't go to the mall with you this afternoon, I've got a couple of chapters to finish in my book."

It will sound silly at first, but it helps to experiment with these lines in the privacy of your bathroom before you try them out on actual people.

❦ Rehearse your scenes.

Now that you've got your props and you know your lines, start acting. If you're playing the role of a professional writer, do what a writer would do. When it's time to schedule a dentist's appointment or a visit with your aunt, look at your calendar and say, "Oh, I can't this week; I've got a deadline hanging over my head."

❧Now go through the motions.

Really say to your best friend, "I can't go shopping, I've got to write," even if you don't have a single word inside you waiting to be written. Really tell the dentist, "I can't get my teeth cleaned until Friday" or "I can't come visit you until next month, Aunt Martha."

Then walk into your closet or attic or basement or the front seat of your car or wherever you've staked out your writing space. Take out your laptop or your notebook and pretend to write.

And the odd thing is that after a while, you make a shift. You stop going through the motions and it starts becoming real. Sooner or later, you may accidentally write something real during your fake sessions. And you'll feel the part. Not only will you start to feel like a real writer, you will actually become one.

That's how this book was born. I was just at the precarious start of my own writing revival when the notion of writing a book for other writers first sidled hesitantly into my brain. "Nah," I said. "That's just a pipe dream. And besides, there are a gazillion-and-one how-to books on writing out there already."

But the idea wouldn't let go, so one morning I decided that I would allow myself to play with it—just for an hour or two, before my next batch of student manuscripts came in for editing. I felt very much like I was only pretending to be serious about this fake book project.

But in going through the motions, something caught fire. Pretend became real, and for the next three days, I wrote non-stop. The 5,000-word essay I'd envisioned mushroomed into a 19,000-word book. It wasn't garbage either. Despite this manic writing pace, what I'd written actually flowed, cohered, made sense.

This is like a real-life version of Natalie Goldberg's freewriting technique. In *Writing Down the Bones*, she recommends sitting down to write for a set period of time each day, even if all you write at first is, "I have nothing to say, I have nothing to say," over and over again.

I'm suggesting that you get up each morning and act like a writer for a set period of time, even if all you accomplish at first is dusting off your keyboard or sharpening your pencils.

If you keep it up, who knows? Sooner or later you might disappear into your new role.

9
WING AND ASH

The natural cycles of a writer's life

It's probably more obvious than I'd like to admit that the impetus for this book was my own pressing need for revival. Raise your hands: how many of you guessed that by page 2?

But more and more lately I wonder. What if these periodic spells of drought, of dearth, of silence aren't the curses we think they are? What if they are gifts instead? If we let them—if we are patient, and don't make the mistake of fleeing our desks for good—these necessary winters can be a source of creative energy.

After all, nature is not dead during the long season of cold and dark, only at rest; below ground roots are burrowing deeper, drawing nourishment from the soil. So it is with writers: not dead to words, just storing up for another summer of growth. This is what makes our writing Januaries a gift.

Nevertheless, the past year of my life, while I was living through it, did not feel much like a gift. It still doesn't. And I'm fairly sure that you don't feel much like celebrating while the days and weeks spool out, and your hands hover over the keyboard, waiting for words that refuse to come.

But out of such difficult, arid months something can flower; it did for me. How much of that came from dogged work—perspiration—and how much came from the enigmatic force of inspiration that I somewhat facetiously keep calling the Muse? That's a mystery we writers will never tease out, I imagine.

All I know is this. In obeying the impulse I had one morning to set aside my paid work for a few hours and "indulge" myself with this pesky book idea, I wrote my way out of my own writer's malaise. In giving what I hope is a gift to other writers, I have given one to myself as well.

It took a series of crises in my life to remind me:

> Take your writing seriously,
> because nobody else will.

It's a distillation, in just eight words, of all the advice I've ever given to my students and clients. And now I'm sharing it with you as well—not because I can claim it as my own, or because I've done such a sterling job of living the advice myself—but because I think so many writers need to hear it. And not just once, but over and over and over again.

We all need to remind ourselves that our writing is something worth doing.

As one of my literary heroes, the neurologist Oliver Sacks, wrote in his book *Hallucinations*:

"To live on a day to day basis is insufficient for human beings; we need to transcend, transport, escape; we need meaning, understanding, and explanation; we need to see overall patterns in our lives."

Reading that yesterday was like discovering the Ba'al Shem Tov quote all over again; it was as if Sacks had seen into my heart. Though my attempts at providing escape, meaning, or transcendence in my books will always fall short, they are still what make the time I spend writing worthwhile.

Have you been able to figure out what makes your writing important to you?

Only then will you be able to spontaneously combust, and from that explosion of creativity write the stories that are burning inside you.

Ultimately, no one can make this revival happen for you. You can read this book, you can absorb the words, you can try the things I've suggested, but only you can stir them to life. There is no magic that will make it happen without effort on your part.

But at the same time, be kind to yourself. You aren't superhuman. There will be times in your life when writing may temporarily seem to take a back seat: births, deaths, weddings, divorces, new jobs, moves, illness, accidents, and so much more can all happen, and will all happen. During those times, you may not be able to devote as much of yourself to writing as you like.

Just remember—even during those fallow times— to respect yourself *as a writer*, to take your work seriously, to realize that the words you write have meaning and worth.

Our writing tribe might want to nominate a British novelist named Barbara Pym as our patron saint. I know, I know—back in chapter 4 when I recommended worshipping a literary hero, I specifically ruled out use of the term saint. But Pym may just qualify.

In the 1950s, Pym published six novels: quietly comic books about the lives of spinsters and curates in English villages. She was well-reviewed, had a body of loyal readers, and seemed to enjoy a solid working relationship with her publisher.

Then in 1963 she submitted her seventh novel— and despite her fans, her good reviews, and her history with the publisher, they refused to print it, saying it was out of step with the times. She revised and resubmitted it, and they rejected it again. She submitted it elsewhere, twenty times. And twenty times it was rejected.

Pym was living through a writer's ultimate nightmare. The people whose opinions she valued—upon whom her very existence as a writer depended—no longer respected her work. She was devastated by this experience. "I get moments of gloom and pessimism when it seems as if nobody could ever like my kind of writing again...." she wrote in 1970.

Note two things about this quote. Though it was seven years after that painful first rejection from her own publisher, Pym was still writing, despite her despair. She continued to believe in the worth and value of her writing even when no one else did. She continued to write.

That's why I've nominated her as our patron saint.

Another nine years went by. Pym was diagnosed with breast cancer and went to live with her sister in a small village, and she continued writing, despite the fact that no one wanted to publish what she wrote.

Bear with me: there is a gloriously happy ending to this tale. In 1977, sixteen years after Pym entered what she called "the wilderness," two other British writers named her as the most under-rated novelist of 20th century England in an article in the London *Times* literary supplement.

It helps to have friends in high places. That same year, Macmillan bought her novel *A Quartet in Autumn* for publication; it made the short list for the Booker Prize. A second novel followed in 1978, and then a US publisher "discovered" her, and all her works were made available for the first time to American readers.

It is Pym's setbacks, not her success, that make her a hero. I call her a literary saint because even in the darkest of times, she was able to show the rest of us the truth and wisdom of this:

Take your writing seriously—even when nobody else does. *Especially* when nobody else does.

So when you can't remember why you're bothering to write, think of Pym.

Even in the grip of the creative rapture that sparked this book, I continued to struggle with moments of doubt. I'd race to my desk every morning, brimming over with ideas and phrases that I couldn't wait to set down. And all day, as long as I kept writing, the dementors kept their distance.

But as soon as the sun started to sink towards the west—I am definitely a morning person when it comes to both productivity and creativity—my well of words would run dry. I'd fall out of what psychologist Mihaly Csikszentmihalyi calls the state of flow.

Our tent revival preacher might use different terminology; he might say that I had fallen from a state of grace.

Whatever it is called, this is how it felt.

—While I was writing, I felt calm and assured that all would be well.

—When I stopped, all the doubt and anxiety burst out of the channels I'd dug for them and flooded me again.

> *Why am I wasting my time writing this book? No one will read it. I've got nothing new or worthwhile to offer. It's all been said a million times before—and said in better prose, too. I'm stupid. I'm a hack. I'm slacking off; I should be applying for that job down at the library.*

And on and on and on the demons fretted and muttered. I imagine you've heard your own version of this corrosive chorus as well.

But for once I took my own advice: you know, what I wrote in chapter 6 about standing my ground while the tide of doubt washed past me. I went for a walk, toasted the sunset with a glass of wine, laughed with my son, and then I slept. Sure, the dementors kept up their nonstop litany of doom in my head, but I turned down the volume and refused to listen.

And every morning I'd wake up refreshed, ready to charge back to my desk.

I admit, after the first few days the whole thing started to feel like a sham. As long as I was caught up in the pure fever of creation, the words steaming out of me, unstoppable, nothing else mattered.

But then groceries would need to be bought, or email from my day job would need to be answered. And I would start to scold myself, "Stop playing around. This so-called book of yours is only a game. Get back to your real work."

I wasn't taking my writing seriously. How could it be important if there was no guarantee that it would ever be read by a single person other than me? How could it be important if it never earned me a single cent?

So I did many of the things I outlined in chapters 4 and 5. I stoked the fire with all the kindling I could scrounge; I hobnobbed, I worshipped, I retreated to my sanctuary. I walked my ritual walk and I drank my ritual tea—and every day these things brought me back to my desk.

To this moment, however, I still feel like I'm playing dress-up—that while I'm parading around in my writer costume, someone out there is going to yank it off and reveal that there's no one under there. I'm not sure if this sense of being a phony—a ghost even—will ever completely go away.

Which is why the single most essential ingredient in my personal bag of revival tricks is this. Do what writers do best: make believe.

So what if my writing sessions feel like a giant game of let's pretend? We are a storytelling species, after all: hard-wired, it seems, to find meaning and purpose through the stories we share. If I have to live out one kind of story…

Once upon a time, there was a woman named Nancy who pretended she was a writer

…for me to write another, then that's what I will continue to do.

Until by pretending to be a writer I realize—I have been one all along.

Know that sometimes it will feel like you are just going through the motions of being a writer, too. You'll have to drag yourself back to your desk over and over again: that's not failure, it is simply part of the cycles of a writer's life. Revival doesn't last forever; eventually whatever is burning when you spontaneously combust is consumed, and you need to replenish it.

And that's all right. Writers need to be like phoenixes, finding a way to take wing no matter how often we taste ash.

SPONTANEOUS COMBUSTION

Seven months after that summer night in my backyard, I was once again outside, shivering a little this time in the chill dusk of a spring evening. Once again I could hear distant words trembling in the air. It was the same preacher, shouting the same words into the same microphone under the same tent.

"Come afire," he said.

And now I'm saying it to you. Come afire.

Be inflamed again with passion for what you do.

Write.

Thank you so much for reading this book.
By now you realize that my so-called credentials
for writing it have less to do with my resumé
than with the hard-won insights I've gleaned
from the day-to-day struggle to keep my own
creative batteries charged.
If you'd like more inspiration to stoke your
writing revival, please join me at

www.nancybutts.com

SPONTANEOUS COMBUSTION

FURTHER READING

Here is a brief and woefully incomplete list of some of the many excellent books available on the crazy craft of writing. What follows are the books I recommend more than any others.

1. Stephen King, *On Writing: A Memoir of the Craft.*

2. John Gardner, *On Becoming a Novelist.*

3. John Gardner, *The Art of Fiction: Notes on Craft for Young Writers.*

4. Ralph Keyes, *The Courage to Write.*

5. Dorothea Brande, *Becoming a Writer.*

6. Brenda Ueland, *If You Want to Write.*

7. Natalie Goldberg, *Writing Down the Bones: Freeing the Writer Within.*

8. Twyla Tharp, *The Creative Habit: Learn It and Use It For Life.*

9. Les Edgerton, *Hooked: Write Fiction That Grabs Readers at Page One & Never Lets Them Go.*

10. Lynne Truss, *Eats, Shoots & Leaves: The Zero Tolerance Approach to Punctuation* [a hilarious and passionate book about the serial comma, of all things].

11. Renni Brown and Dave King, *Self-Editing for Fiction Writers.*

12. Alice W. Flaherty, *The Midnight Disease: The Drive to Write, Writer's Block, and the Creative Brain.*

13. Anne Lamott, *Bird by Bird.*

14. And of course, William Strunk Jr. and EB White [of *Charlotte's Web* fame], *The Elements of Style*.

ABOUT THE AUTHOR

Nancy Butts published her first poem at the age of ten and has been writing ever since. An award-winning newspaper writer and editor, she was able to make the leap to her true love, fiction, with the publication of two YA novels, *Cheshire Moon* and *The Door in the Lake*, which was an ALA Quick Pick and a Scholastic Book Club selection.

She was the lead editor of a non-fiction book on revision by Sandy Asher entitled *Writing it Right!* She has taught writing for thirteen years at the Institute of Children's Literature, and has also led writing workshops both at SCBWI conferences and at community colleges.

She is a *magna cum laude* graduate of Duke University—and a one-time *Jeopardy* champion.

A frequent contributor to education textbooks, she has published five books for the classroom under her own name. She loves to work individually with writers as an editor and manuscript consultant to help them achieve their dreams of publishing a book.

You can find out more at her website.

www.nancybutts.com